COMPLICATED ALLIANCES: ACCOUNTS OF CAREER WOMEN OF THE U.S. ARMED FORCES & WOMEN WHO LOVE MEN IN THE U.S. ARMED FORCES

PRESENTED BY

DR. KAREN HILLS PRUDEN

Copyright © 2021 by Dr. Karen Hills Pruden

Pruden Global Business Solutions Consulting, LLC

Virginia Beach, Virginia

All rights reserved. This book or any portion thereof may not be reproduced or used in any manner whatsoever without the express written permission of the publisher except for the use of brief quotations in a book review.

Printed in the United States of America

First Printing, 2021

ISBN: 9798710377895

Ordering Information:

Quantity sales. Special discounts are available on quantity purchases by corporations, associations, and others who purchase directly from the publisher.

Contact: admin@drkarenhillspruden.com

Book Cover: Purple Inc. Marketing

Editing: Simene Walden

TABLE OF CONTENTS

Introduction..6

Distance Makes the Marriage Stronger

Katrina S. Tasby…………………………………..9

Adventures of a Military Spouse

Beth Howell……………………………………17

Loving Through Your Complicated Alliance

Deborah Juniper-Frye……………………………25

The Polites' Quiet Storm

Delores Pruitt-Polite……………………………40

Tied Migrant and Career Woman

Dr. Denise Robertson-Lambert………………...48

A Country Girl Who Believed She Could

S'Estlavie Kaschan Bridges……………………58

Behold the One Percenter

Dr. Zakiya O. Mabery…………………………66

A Sea Bag, Dog Tags, and Love Saved Me

Tamika Quinn…………………………………74

Switched Navy Career Three Times, Found My Calling

Theresa Carpenter……………………………..84

THE VISIONARY

Dr. Karen Hills Pruden is a dual executive who works as the Chief Human Resource Officer and the Founder of Pruden Global Business Solutions Consulting. She is known as the ***Career Elevation Expert*** for women middle managers aspiring to senior leadership positions because she demystifies the senior leadership role through coaching programs, online classes, books and speaking engagements.

An award-winning human resource executive, she has been recognized by the governor of Virginia for her work in Equity, Diversity, and Inclusion. In 2020, she was listed as one of the Most Influential African Americans on LinkedIn. She is a Certified Diversity Executive, a 10X author, with six books reaching #1 on Amazon Bestsellers List.

Associated Social Media sites (Dr. Karen Hills Pruden):

Website: http://www.drkarenhillspruden.com/

Conference Website: http://www.sisterleadersconference.com

LinkedIn: https://www.linkedin.com/in/dr-karen-hills-pruden-dm-sphr-3935626a/

Instagram: https://www.instagram.com/DrKarenHillsPruden/

Amazon Author Central: https://www.amazon.com/Dr.-Karen-Hills-Pruden/e/B08D8LRPT3?ref_=dbs_p_ebk_r00_abau_000000

INTRODUCTION
BY
DR. KAREN HILLS PRUDEN

Full disclosure, I am passionate about women and the U.S. Armed Forces. Like several of the authors in this anthology, I come from a military family. My father is a veteran of the U.S. Army. He was stationed in the very area where I live now. His assignment here, led to him meeting my mother. They married and the rest is history.

My brother and my sister joined the U.S. Army. Their decisions may have been partially based on my dad's time in the Armed Forces. My sister retired from the Army after dedicating almost two decades. And then there is me. I originally planned to enter the military after high school. A medical situation prevented my enlistment. I went on to college and later married a retired U.S. Army veteran.

Even with my familial ties to the military, I was unaware of the impact the U.S. Armed Forces could have on a woman's career until I moved into leadership in human resources. During my two-decade career I have had exhausting battles with managers simply in my advocating for them to give a female applicant, who had gaps on her resume, a chance. *"Bring her in and give her a chance to tell you about the gaps"*, I would say. *"Do not just dismiss her."* I would plead. My never-ending battles are where the concept of **COMPLICATED ALLIANCES** was birthed.

This anthology tells the experiences of four active-duty military, four women who love/loved men in the U.S. Armed Forces and one woman veteran who is also a wife of a U.S. veteran. These nine women reflected in their own words, the **COMPLICATED ALLIANCES** between career, family, and loyalty to a country they admired and love. The common thread among the women's experiences is that each woman relied on some form of help.

This help came in various forms. Family relationships were critical. However, relationships with friends were more constant. Many times, military deployments moved these women out of the physical reach of family. One consequence of the **COMPLICATED ALLIANCE** between the women who loved men in the U.S. Armed Forces was whether she would move with her spouse during deployment. There were consequences whether the woman moved or stayed.

For the woman who moved with her spouse, that notification to move could be effective in a matter of days. Within days she may be unemployed, and thrust into the logistics of moving the family to the next duty station. Once she arrives at the new location, finding a job at her desired career level may prove difficult. The short stints of employment on her resume due to tied migration may cause potential employers to question her stability. *Tied migration is when one spouse moves for employment and the other spouse follows.*

For the woman who chooses not to move with her spouse she may experience another set of issues. Although she is able to continue her career, bouts of loneliness and resentment of parenting alone may plague the couple. Long distance relationships can be an emotional and financial strain on the couple. When military hops are not available, the costs to shuffle to and from separate locations to see one another can substantially cripple a couple's finances.

I am excited to be the conduit to allow these women to tell their story. Whether the woman is/was a service member or the spouse of a service member, these women are truly heroic for navigating the **COMPLICATED ALLIANCE** between family, and career.

KATRINA S. TASBY

DISTANCE MAKES THE MARRIAGE STRONGER

I still remember the day we met...well at least the month; April 2002. His warm smile is what first attracted me to him. He stood there strikingly tall in his dress blues, shaking my hand a few seconds longer than he should have. A mutual friend introduced us, and at the time I was still Active-Duty Air Force. A budding friendship turned into more by August of that year. Fast forward to August 2006, I separated from the U.S. Air Force after serving 8 ½ years. The following month, after a long day of work and going to class for one of my degree, he surprised me by proposing. I had no idea this was coming. Yes, we were together for 4 years by this point. However, I was in shock. It was around 10 pm. I was trying to eat my Wendy's nuggets and get ready for bed all at the same time. He was busy trying to get my attention by grabbing my hand. I looked at him with the look we ladies can give when we get annoyed, but I finally gave in to see what was up. When I realized what was going on, I hurriedly chewed my food to give him my undivided attention. He wanted to spend the rest of his life with me! After I wiped the crumbs from my mouth, we sealed the deal. He then told me he planned to ask me during a romantic dinner that weekend, but he could not contain himself. We were married in June of 2007. The following year which was January 2008 is when he took a job doing Legislative Affairs for the Secretary of the Air Force.

We were based out of the Washington D.C. area and this great opportunity came for my husband to take an assignment as a Legislative Liaison. At the time, I knew it would be a great opportunity that could set him up for retirement. I'm always forward-thinking. However, what I didn't think about was how much time he would spend away from home. At first, he was just going to work on Capitol Hill like any normal day. One day a week he would be in his dress blues. The other days he would wear civilian clothes, a suit, and tie. My favorite look for my husband is his navy-blue suit with his light blue shirt, white collar, white sleeve cuff, a pair of cufflinks, and a blue paisley tie. As you can see, I have an affinity to see my husband in blue. He wears the color well. Soon the days would get longer with him working long hours, and then came his first trip. I tried to be strong before he left, but I cried a little. That first night I cried like a big baby. It was tough just knowing he was in some far-off county and the fear of the unknown ravaged my mind. That was the longest 5 days ever. What I didn't know, I had more of a struggle to come.

A few months into this assignment and a few trips later, his two sons came to live with us permanently. Raising two young teenage sons while my husband was away, was tough. They acted out in various ways. I was often told, "you are not my mom". As time went on, we found our way. One thing I never did was treat them like they were stepchildren. I always treated them like how I was raised, with all the love and care in the world. Another mom on the base asked me how I did it. How did I treat my boys the way I did? I told her; I treat them as if they were my biological children. I went on to tell her that I did not see a difference between children and stepchildren; either way they are my sons. She looked at me dumbfounded because of the way she dealt with her stepson versus how she showed love and affection to her biological children. After that conversation, that emphasized to me that I was going in the right direction with raising my young princes.

As I said, we got into our routine. We were used to my husband being on travel for a week then coming home for two days then on travel again. It was like that for almost five years. Missed birthdays, missed three-day weekends when we would go out of town, missed Valentine's Day, and missed anniversaries were our new normal. I remember one day after I left work, I went to a hair appointment, went to one son's basketball game, and left there to get to the other one's wrestling match. The one son that did wrestled did not believe that I saw him. Let me tell you, I made it just in time to see him. I recounted everything I saw. From when he walked onto the mat, to everything he did in his match. All to prove that I saw him. That wasn't the first or last time that happened.

There were days that I was stretched thin with little time for fun. So, when I had time, I would hang out with friends in Georgetown, Old Town Alexandria, or other parts of Washington, DC. One of the boys would call to check on me, then ask, "Can you send a pizza?" If I knew I was going to be out, I would leave money for the bowling alley so they could get food from there.

I was the one that saw my oldest son off to prom while my husband was in some other country. He had to settle for pictures after he returned home. I taught them how to drive. I would have one of them drive down George Washington Parkway. They would drive so close to the right side I thought we were going to end up in a ditch. I would hit my imaginary brake while teaching them to parallel park in Old Town Alexandria in random neighborhoods. The other one son would drive back. After a few times driving with them I found a driving school. I couldn't take it; the whole process was nerve-racking.

Throughout those years we had some complicated times. I thought about how my husband being away affected me and the boys. I never really thought about how it affected my husband until his retirement ceremony in January 2013. The Speaker of the House presided over his ceremony on Capitol Hill. She said such great things about him. After the ceremony, bipartisan members of Congress all told me something special about my husband and how he spoke of his family. Some of his past supervisors from that job were in attendance as well as Generals and Colonels. They all spoke very highly of him and expressed to me how much his family, meant to him. At that moment I knew it was just as hard for him as it was for us.

I had imagined him as this jet setter traveling to all these countries where under normal circumstances he would never go to. I knew it would be rough on him. I just did not think of it in that way. He still hasn't slept through the night unless he is sick. All the travel between the varying time zones for those five years has taken its toll on him.

All the countries were not so great. So, I knew it was not all unicorns and rainbows. I was low-key jealous of the position he had or maybe just the traveling part. He always brought me back something from each country. That is where my affection for hand-painted leaves or feathers came from. I have two beautiful hand-painted leaves from India that may just be my favorite pieces. Also, he brought back a bottle of red and a bottle of white wine from each country, the reason why I love a good Argentinian Malbec. (why does the love it) I am still promised to go to a few of those places. To this day, my husband hates to be away from home. Dare I say it? He hates being away from me.

In 2015, I applied for a position that I thought was in the Washington, DC area. It wasn't until I got an interview and was selected that I noticed it was in Houston, TX. He told me to take the position. "I've already had my career, now it is your time."

That meant the world to me that he now put me and my career first. I moved to Houston in November 2015. We were back to traveling since he was still working in Crystal City, VA. I would fly home twice a month and he would come to Houston on the weekends that I couldn't get back home. It took us back to when he was working on Capitol Hill. Finally, in June 2016, my husband left his job and moved to Houston permanently. I told you, he hates to be away from me.

Bio:

Katrina Tasby is a U.S. Air Force Veteran who resides in the greater Houston, Texas area. After moving to Houston in 2015 for a promotion with the Federal Government, Mrs. Tasby felt she wanted more for herself and her family. A few years later, she studied to become a realtor and obtained her real estate license. Next, with her husband the two of them started their own business, The Art of Cleaning Services, LLC. They are a Service-Disabled Veteran-Owned Small Business. Katrina is a business owner in her own right. Katrina has her MBA and a Master's Degree in Project Management. She is married to her wonderful husband, Marvin who is Retired, U.S. Air Force. Together they enjoy playing golf, traveling, watching movies, and spending time with family and friends. She is a bonus mom to wonderful boys, one who followed in the family footsteps and joined the military.

WOMEN

WHO LOVE MEN

IN THE

UNITED STATES ARMED FORCES

BETH HOWELL

ADVENTURES OF
A MILITARY SPOUSE – CONTRAILS

I have had many adventures during this military spouse life! Where do contrails come in? Think of ever-changing pathways! The ability to "go with the flow." What was known yesterday does not exist today; although, it can have permanent impact. Take orders for one example, Chris, my hubby, had orders to Washington, D.C. We were excited. Then, six weeks out from the move, instead of Washington, D.C., the orders changed to Langley Air Force Base in southeast Virginia. While both are on the east coast, the locations (and opportunities for a working spouse) are very different. At least, we had six weeks to change everything, to include our mindsets. We had friends who shared that they had never been to Hawaii, but their furniture had! They were en route when the orders changed. They ended up going to Alaska instead! The running joke became "Don't answer the phone!" Of course, there were other jokes too about Assignments. Like Assignments officers playing darts while blindfolded and drinking.

I am a positive person and have obtained resilience through my experiences. Let us talk about the downs first and get them out of the way. As a career woman, my potential earning power and lifetime earnings have been significantly impacted. I get the occasional call about a Human Resources Vice President role. However, I had those same calls twenty years ago and could not take the opportunities. Opportunities were in one place … the base assignment was in another.

Now for the positives! We can start with travel! We have friends who have lived all over the world in lovely locations such as Germany and Belgium. Our most exotic locations were Louisiana and New Mexico. It depends on what the spouse's role is, as to where you may be able to go. Certain planes are only in certain locations. Take your pick: very hot or very cold!

When my hubby, Chris, transferred into a different role, we went to New Mexico. Since we knew it was a two-year assignment, we made a list of everything we wanted to see and do. Then, we transferred the list to the calendar. By doing so, we did not have to spend time when the weekend rolled around figuring out what we were going to do! We completed most of our list. I have pictures of Tiffany, our baby girl, now a college student, crawling through the sands of White Sands National Park. Blake, Sammy, Matt, and Tiffany enjoyed going to Carlsbad Caverns! Two highlights for the kids come to mind: 1) eating 750 feet underground at the snack bar (they found that fascinating); and 2) watching the bats come out of the cave! Way back then, I was thankful there was an elevator back to the top. Today, I run marathons and I am an avid hiker. We have lived relatively close to a beach; near the mountains and in the middle of what felt like nowhere.

I owe my resilience level to being a military spouse. While I have seen disappointments and felt them too during the pandemic of 2020, the military spouse life changed my way of thinking. The last time Chris deployed, we had a seven-day window to prepare … a Monday-to-Monday scenario, which started the week of Thanksgiving. In that seven days, we celebrated Thanksgiving, Christmas, Blake's birthday (January 9th), our anniversary (February 14th) / Valentine's Day, and Easter. A day is a day is a day. While we would all love to celebrate on a particular day in a specific way, the reality is that it has not always been possible. We have learned to make the best of a situation. We also updated our wills and had family portraits made. It is amazing how much can get done when the "GO" button is pressed. The "GO" button mentality has impacted me in every area of my life. I have been skydiving, ziplining, and white-water rafting. I am a fairly adventurous soul!

When our youngest was a teen, I was able to start accepting opportunities. I maintained a separate household in a couple of different states over a five-year period. I went where needed, when needed, and in whatever capacity or role was needed. Often on short notice! This way of life holds true for me today too! When I worked for a large defense contractor, I was interviewed on a Thursday to leave the next Tuesday for three months. I enjoyed my time in Alaska working with military programs on Fort Wainwright! I also enjoyed seeing the Northern Lights, going north of the Arctic Circle, and landing on a glacier on Denali. Another time, I was in Costa Rica serving on a turtle conservation project while on vacation. I returned from vacation late Saturday. On Sunday, when I was checking my emails, I ended up making calls to find out I was moving from Virginia to South Carolina … and leaving on Tuesday. Did I panic? No! On Monday, I jumped into high gear, let my team know I was transferring, started handing off work, and packed up my office. That is where the "GO" button comes in. Military members and their families make it happen. Whatever it is. We find a path. We make a way.

As an adventure seeker, I applied for Riyadh and Cairo only to find out on a Friday afternoon that I would not be receiving either adventure. The role for Riyadh went to someone who had been there to work before. The role for Cairo went to someone who had lived there for twenty years. I chomped on sour grapes and maybe even privately pouted for all of about five minutes. Yes, I was disappointed, but the reality is that we only have so much life. Unless we can find a way to energize the disappointment into action, our best strategy is to move on. Move on, I did. I looked for an opportunity to go skydiving. As with working internationally, skydiving was on my bucket list! The very next day, I jumped out of a perfectly good airplane! Going skydiving was within my control ... right up until the moment I stepped out of the aircraft! And, yes, I have now done that more than once!

Another positive that comes to mind is the source of "instant" friendships. Within the military spouse community, there are various clubs. I had the pleasure of serving on the board for multiple clubs. My favorite is the Air Force Officers' Spouses' Club of Washington, D.C. I served as the Special Activities Co-Chair for two years and it has been my favorite role, aside from serving on the Air Force Charity Ball Committee as Treasurer. I love sharing adventures with our members; many of whom are international. Working and living internationally remains high on my bucket list. I enjoy learning about other cultures and getting to know people from around the world. I have friends from

Scotland, Belgium, India, Thailand, Singapore, Algeria, Argentina, Chile, Japan, Lithuania, and many other countries! We develop lifelong friendships and some of us have grown so close that we consider ourselves "sisters for life." This sisterhood is important to me. These ladies are my positive, supportive cheering section whether I am local or residing around the globe. Strong women build each other up! We are human resources directors, architects, real estate agents, teachers, professors, doctors, and travel associates, amidst many other careers. We are military spouses, sisters for life, friends, and confidents.

Has this life always been easy? No. Has it always gone according to plan? Most definitely not! Yet, it has been good. With the challenges have come opportunities. My life did not turn out as planned. That is what can happen when you marry someone in a flight suit. Are there things I wish I could change? Sure. I think we all have those. That being said, we all know the past is history and behind us. How we picture the history is as important as how we manage the present and plan for the future. We do what we can with what we have, and hope for the best. It is a mindset. We can focus on the regrets or challenges or we can focus on the positive. As a military spouse, I choose the positive.

As a Personnel Specialist in the U.S. Air Force Reserves who served during my college years, I learned about the military before marrying into it. Being so young with responsibility made a difference in my life. I was the last person to go over the DD-93 (Record of

Emergency Data – who gets the benefits) with service members in my reserve unit before they deployed! I have carried that sense of responsibility with me throughout my life, in my career, and in my marriage. We find a way. We make it happen. Make no mistake. The service member may be the one in uniform, but the family is along for the flight. Let us press the "GO" button, take flight, and make some contrails! **Go Air Force!**

Bio:

Beth Howell is a human resources, management and administration professional with experience covering diverse corporations with a global presence. While at Global 500 and Fortune 500 multi-national organizations Beth partnered with stakeholders in countries across the Americas, United Kingdom, Europe, Middle East, and South-Central Asia. Beth has been a key leader of human capital practices, compliance, and global technology solutions. She specializes in building relationships down the hall or around the world.

Beth holds Senior Professional in Human Resources (SPHR) and Senior Certified Professional (SHRM-SCP) certifications. She earned a Bachelor of Arts in Psychology from Huntingdon College in Montgomery, AL, USA, and a Master of Business Administration from the University of New Mexico in Albuquerque, NM, USA.

Beth has held numerous leadership positions in military spouse, human resources, and equal opportunity organizations, serving in roles which usually have relationship building, regeneration, outreach, STEM, and / or philanthropy as a focus.

www.linkedin.com/in/bethhowellbipw

DEBORAH JUNIPER-FRYE

LOVING THROUGH YOUR COMPLICATED ALLIANCE

Complicated ~ someone or something that is hard to understand or something that is hard to untangle; a romantic relationship that involves more. www.yourdictionary.com

Complicated Alliances.......

Alliance ~ a relationship forged between two or more individuals or groups that works as a positive for both parties involved.
www.yourdictionary.com

Complicated Alliances ~ what a title and topic! This little country girl here has surely seen some complicated alliances throughout my 35-year marriage with my Serviceman and now, U. S. Navy Retired Veteran. Being a military brat, I took a vow that I would never date or marry anyone that worked on a military base, let alone, someone who was actually enlisted in the military. But, low and behold, on a Friday night in December of 1986, my subdued life changed forever. It sure did, and I must say, for the better.

Listen, in an effort to get over a terrible break-up from a five-year relationship, my sister and her best friend invited me to go out dancing. As I was out on the dance floor, throwing down and releasing some stress, I glanced over to the side, and there stood this tall and handsome guy. This was at a popular local night club called the Fox Trap and the DJ played dynamic music for forty-five minutes at a time. But wait, when I turned around again, there he was, still standing and now obviously staring and what the younger generation now calls, stalking. It was so cute but annoying at the same time. Because remember, I was getting over a bad breakup, right? As my sister Sharon and I were walking back to our table, she whispers, "Deborah, that guy is following you". I distinctly remember saying, "I'm not in the mood for this and I'm going to use him like I had been used". So, I thought. Up walks this handsome, deep voiced gentleman named Michael Frye, who pursued me in a way that made me feel somewhat giddy. It was a sure bet that after I told him about me being a single mother, he would surely get lost, because most men don't want to become an instant Dad. However, Michael was such a different man unlike those that I previously encountered. His kindness and sincere heart set him apart in so many ways and this girl was tickled pink that he was choosing me. It was such an unexpected mutual and surreal experience that it took a hold of us immediately and from that day forward we became best friends and fell in love. Approximately 120 days later, we said, "I Do" and from the time we met in December until getting married in April of the following year, it was like a match made in Heaven. You see, when Michael came along, it was my first time of experiencing such devotion and tender priority. When we first met, it was Michael's thoughtfulness that created a smile on my face and warmth in my heart that I had never felt before. It was such an unexpected, sweet sight to see him parked in front of my Mom's house, waiting for me to get home so he could greet and assist me with whatever I needed. Now, that may sound very insignificant to many, but for me, it was huge. But let us move on so I can get to more of that later.

The first man that loved and adored me was also a U. S. Navy Serviceman that retired after serving our country for more than twenty-six years. He was an Aircraft Technician and he was my Dad. Back during that time, we could be assured that his daily life abroad and stateside was full of complex racial division. My daddy was a man of one wife, ten children. He worked tirelessly around the clock to be a great sailor, father, and husband; even if it was from a distance most of the time, due to his military obligation. But as you can see, Juke & Corrine made the best of their time together, almost adding a new child every other year. It wasn't until I was up in age that I realized the significance of daddy's sacrifice for us and it wasn't until he passed away, that a flood of dormant memories resurfaced to soothe my heart and help me through my traumatic grief. The first memory was finding a gold mine stumbling across my dad's military cruise books from the various ships and duty stations that he was assigned that included his entire military file and letters of accommodation. So, to those reading this that still have your dad around, love him and cherish every moment. If you don't have a good relationship with your dad or no matter how complex it is, try your best to make it better. I always say that God has a way of bringing some good out of grief. I married a man who has the same birthday as my daddy which is January 10th! This day has become a day of celebration for my husband and honor for my dad. Sometimes complexity can become sweet.

Whoa, wait a minute! Did I say I went from being a single mother to getting married to a stranger within 120 days? Now this was a "complicated alliance" to the tenth degree. I didn't know anything about being a wife; let alone a military spouse. Listen, I just learned how to be a responsible parent; Michael had just left his ex-girlfriend in CT and on top of that, he was on sea duty. It was a mess wrapped up in grace! And wait, did I mention that I did not meet my in-laws until after we got married at the Justice of the Peace? Michael teases me all the time, saying "It was a shotgun wedding". We had a reception at our townhouse a week later and then Michael took me to his hometown to meet his parents. LOL, a mess wrapped up in grace. I tell you we had so many ups and downs in our young marriage that we didn't know whether we were coming or going.

With Michael being on sea duty, the first few years were filled with three days on, three days off duty, tiger cruises, 6-month cruises, and even an 18-month deployment to another state. Yes, we lived apart for 18 months. When he was out to sea on long deployments, there were so many days when I would look up at the sky and so many nights when I would look up at the stars and wonder "Where is my husband, what is he doing, and who is he with?" I will never forget the moment when the breaking news banner ran across the CNN News Station that broadcasted a Russian Ship run into a U.S. Navy Ship, realizing that was the USS Caron where Michael was stationed on. The horror of witnessing the two ships collide in the middle of a massive sea was just indescribable. May I say, our servicemen and women deserve honor, appreciation and respect, as they constantly put themselves in harm's way, while being our gatekeepers of land, air, and sea.

As a career woman who loves a man in the U.S. Armed Forces, your life, goals, and aspirations can be swept away and somewhat out of reach. When Michael and I met and fell in love, my five year stay at Old Dominion University had just taken off and the career path had already been mapped out with a targeted plan of retiring as an Old Dominion University Alumni and Staffer. And with no warning, he comes home to say, "Honey, our next duty station will be overseas in Italy or Spain, which one do you want? Neither!!!

I had never been away from home. Norfolk was all I knew and to now be moving to another country, Rota, Spain, seemed inconceivable. The thought of me leaving my career, my dysfunctional life, and all of the chaos to go and explore the possibility of a better life was not something I mapped out. Our family was growing; Antione was nine years old, and Michael Jr. was almost a year in age. I had to put my selfish ways aside and I thought about the possibilities of just maybe, just maybe adapting to the unknown with a new mindset. With me now being a Grief Recovery Method Specialist, I can look back and say that during this life-changing transitional move, we were experiencing emotional grief and trauma. To be pulled away from all you know and take up residence in another whole country was unimaginable at the time. I will never forget the sadness on my son's face, my broken heart of leaving my mom, and even the countenance my husband had because he too was leaving his family. Let me tell you, I became my own worst enemy. We were blessed with a beautiful furnished five-bedroom brick home in Puerto de Santa Maria in the province of Vista Hermosa. There were lovely orange trees in the front and back yard; marble counter tops and flooring all throughout the house, a lovely patio, and guess what, I was miserable. We had one vehicle to get around and Michael was away quite often with his new 1st Class role and increased supervisory duties. Like I said, I was my own worst enemy and my husband had no idea who he was coming home to. It could be his wife Deborah or the woman who was full of anger and plotting to divorce him with plans to leave in the middle of the night.

The situation was a mess wrapped up in grace I tell you. God had a secret in the fine print that I never saw before going to Rota, Spain. The joke was on me. I could not leave Spain unless accompanied by Michael and he already told me, he wasn't taking me anywhere. I'm so confident that it was at that point when God said, "Let me help this fool". No joke, it was an epiphany moment; a moment of sudden revelation and insight to see what was really happening. Things started turning around for our family, the children were happy and adapting very well, Michael was advancing with influence on his job, and we received our new apartment back on the base in USA housing. What a blessing. I was getting back to my right mind and creating a home for our children and we settled in nicely. We started having daily adventures driving through the streets of Rota, hunting down the man to get butano for warming the house, and going to the market in town for fresh fruits and veggies. Fresh, just picked from a tree or pulled from the ground. We would play ping pong in our backyard while the children picked delicious oranges from the tree. My favorite place to meet Michael for lunch was a place called Rascals on base. Things and situations that were once so complicated, became a joy. No matter how crazy or irrational my behavior became, Michael was always so supportive in giving me space and caring for all of us in a way that truly displayed his unwavering and unconditional love.

Although Michael worked around the clock, he found time to pour back into the youth as a Little League Baseball, Basketball, and Football Coach. Our son Antione would outrun, out hit, and outshoot other players, earning him a spot on the European All-Star Baseball Team, two year in a row. But with highs also comes some lows. I remember so vividly that Coach Frye had to endure racial injustice and attacks from jealous parents, because he had the winning teams every year. Things had become so bad during a baseball game with him being heckled from angry parents that the children were actually confused to what they were witnessing. Of course, this was the one game that I didn't attend, but I felt something in my gut and asked Michael to behave himself before they left the house for the game. Wouldn't you know it, this was the game that tipped the scale for Coach Frye and the game ended with one parent being punched in the face and Coach Frye heading to the Police Station to turn himself in. Needless to say, he had no more trouble out of that guy.

As a person who has been employed since my early teenage years, I was ecstatic when offered employment at the Morale, Welfare, and Recreation Department (MWR) in Rota, Spain. My immediate supervisor was Mr. Antonio Navarro and my director was Steven Endres, who spoke fluent Spanish as we Americans walked in. LOL!

On this job, I was responsible for the message traffic which RM1 Frye was in charge of at the Communications Center. The role of Office/Executive Assistant gave me the opportunity to collaborate with high-ranking military personnel and numerous organizations throughout the base and out in town. Life was so good. We had a Spanish babysitter and gardener; our corner apartment was the playground for so many of the neighborhood children and we showed love to each and every one of them. One of our many highlights while living in Spain was the birth of our baby girl, Whitney. Our amazing family was growing and it included Antione, Michael Jr., Whitney, and our new puppy, Kimba. Additional highlights included our many trips and travels to places like Gibraltar, Torremolinos, Germany, and Morocco to name a few. Would you believe that our number one place to eat was called, "Chicken in the Dirt"? When taking a hard pivot of my thoughts and looking back, it is clear that no matter what vessel or command Michael was attached to, what base he worked on, or which quarterdeck he stood watch, he was a natural born leader. He grew in favor and became a mentor to so many and managed to have some of those life-long friends, still to this day. No matter the location, he found himself being selected to be the Leading Petty Officer (LPO) to oversee, manage, and coordinate the day-to-day operations of what was then called, the Radio Shack. RMI Frye has shared so many stories of courage, love, and unity. Yet he shared even more stories of heartache and unfairness within his twenty years of faithful military service. As we have grew older, we have chalked those things up to be LIFE; some good and some bad, but yet we have learned how to live, laugh, and love through this journey.

Live ~ Let your light so shine before men. Matthew 5:16

Laugh ~ A time to weep and a time to laugh. Ecclesiastes 3:4

Love ~ That ye love one another, as I have loved you. John 13:34

Right here, can I just say that I LOVE my Serviceman! We had our ups and down but it was nothing compared to our commitment to one another. In my husband's career, he spent 11 years, 6 months, and 3 days on sea duty and quite a bit of time away on shore duty as well. Therefore, this girl here had to come up with all sorts of things to remain closely tied to my boyfriend even when he was a million miles away. As he sailed on the high seas for six months, I would write a letter every night before going to bed. When I did not have too much to say, it was a simple note with "I Love You" kissed with his favorite red lipstick and a spritz of his favorite perfume. Those were some of the best times sending him home movies, music videos that was then packaged as a VHS with his favorite treats and goodies. And it was enough for him to share with those who didn't get mail and packages that often. When we lived apart for eighteen months, with Michael in Louisiana and me in Virginia, we maintained communication through phone calls and once a month weekend military hops. During this time apart, Michael was reassigned yet again to a staff unit in Bahrain/Persian Gulf, to be a part of the mine countermeasure group. Although this was a stressful time for us, we were blessed by him being promoted to First Class Petty Officer. I can go on and on with so many obstacles we endured and overcame, but ultimately love, respect, and keeping each other as a priority, got us through.

Lessons that I've Learned

- *Stay spiritually grounded and maintain a prayer life.*
- *Seek counsel from trusted friends and loved ones.*
- *Be creative in your thinking and keep a can-do mentality.*
- *Live life to the fullest and be each other's #1 Fan.*
- *Make each other a priority and cherish each other in words and deeds.*

Our career twilight begins with final orders back to the states and we were looking forward and preparing for retirement time! Apprehension and anxiety all fell into play, as we were faced once again with a career move. We found ourselves relying on one another even more as we began the transition from military to civilian life. I often get asked the question, "if you could do it all over again, what would you do different?" That question I ponder before answering because most of us would like to think we got everything right the first time. As I reflect, I wonder where we would be if we had taken the option to reside and retire overseas? What life would look like if we had chosen another state to live in. You know what, we are content with the hand we were dealt and the life cards we played. We have come a long way with our "Complicated Alliances" and call ourselves blessed as we journey on in Love, Faith, and Committed Resilience.

I dedicate this poem to all of the HONORABLE Servicemen, who have etched amazing memories on my heart forever beginning with my amazing husband, Michael A. Frye (U. S. Navy Retired); my dedicated dad, Francis A. Juniper (U. S. Navy Retired); my courageous father-in-love, Herbert Frye (U. S. Navy); my supportive brother, Frederick A. Juniper (U. S. Army); and my loyal brother-in-love, Dennis S. Frye (U.S. Marine Corps Retired).

"A SAILOR YOU BE"

By Noel Payne

Have you felt salt spray, upon your face?

Have you seen porpoise at the bow, keeping pace?

Have you viewed sea birds, above the wake in flight?

Have you fixed on a star, at sunset shining bright?

Has there been a time, to save a shipmate?

Has the roll of the deck, ever kept you awake?

Has the vastness of sea, left you feeling alone?

Has a foreign port, made you wish you were home?

If you have weighed anchor, from calm shelter

If you have crossed the equator, at noon time swelter

If you have stood your watch, on a pitching deck

If you have made landfall, on the horizon a speck

When you have secured the decks, for the night to turn in

When you have mustered at sunrise, seen a new day begin

When you have dogged down hatched, in mountainous sea

When you have known all these things, a sailor you be.

Bio: As a longtime Grief Specialist, Deborah Frye has worked with countless families and organizations through the grief process, to gain understanding, new hope, and self-awareness. She has also witnessed, endured, and overcame the stress and trauma that comes with grief or deep sadness.

Deborah is the business owner of Grief Care Consulting LLC and the author of two books, "Grieving Under Grace" and "What About Me? I'm Sad Too." which is a children's grief activity book. She is an Ambassador for the When Women Talk (#WWT) Organization and a Grief Recovery Method Specialist through the Grief Recovery Institute. She has taken additional certificate courses at Yale University, Johns Hopkins University, and the Cognitive Behavior Institute.

Deborah has lived abroad as a military wife, resides in Virginia Beach, VA, and has been madly in love with her husband, Michael for over thirty-five years. They have three adult children; Antione, Michael, Jr., and Whitney, as well as, three grandchildren, Antione, Jr., Aaliyah, and Raevyn.

DELORES PRUITT-POLITE

THE POLITES' QUIET STORM

Sunrays

Maya Angelou said it best. We delight in the beauty of the butterfly, but rarely admit the changes it has gone through to achieve that beauty. It was a hot summer Sunday in 1996. I took my son Berice to Norfolk's Northside Park to play at the newly constructed children's play area. It was playtime for him and playtime for mommy. As a single parent working two jobs, Sundays after church was the only spare time I had for leisure. Sundays at Northside Park was well known in Hampton

Roads as a spot to gather and socialize and possibly meet new people. I was single and ready to mingle!

Everyone would wash and wax their cars and show off their best summer attire. I took special care in selecting my favorite jean shorts with the matching top purchased from the then popular retailer Merry Go Round. I paid a whopping $88 for the outfit months prior. This Sunday was the perfect opportunity to strut in my new attire. Berice played his heart out at the playground as usual, working up an appetite. He pointed across the street to the infamous two golden arches saying mommy, "Can we please go there!" McDonald's happy meal and ice cream cone were his favorite. I recall counting the change on the counter praying I had enough money to satisfy my four-year-old's request. Payday was not until Friday. Berice was finishing up his ice cream cone as we stood on the side of the Mc Donald's building taking in the atmosphere.

A tall exceptionally handsome gentleman looked at me, leaned in, and asked softly, "Is he your son?" I replied, "Yes." He said, "Nice, you are pretty". My name is Earl Polite. "May I call you sometime?" My stomach was in knots. I replied, "Give me your number and I will call you". He said with confidence, "You might want to call me, I have it made for life." I thought to myself; is he a basketball player, football player, or a rapper? I focused in on his features attempting to see if I recognized him from television or magazines. I asked, "What do you do?" He said, "I am in the United States Navy. I would like to take you and your son out to dinner." My smile was bright as a ray of sunlight. I graciously accepted his invitation.

The Eclipse

"Love is patient, love is kind. It does not envy, it does not boast, it is not proud." (1 Corinthians 13:4) After dating for several months. Earl and I fell in love! We searched for an apartment to share and began cohabitating. We had big plans for our future together. Earl was constantly deployed for weeks, often months at a time. In the beginning it was exciting. When the ship docked, Earl would call me from all over the world; Turkey, Spain, Venezuela, Brazil to name a few ports. He would return home baring gifts from beautiful destinations. They say absence makes the heart grow fonder. I found no lies in that statement. The writing of letters, late night phone calls, and welcome home pier side celebrations left room for creativity in our relationship. The excitement soon faded as the reality of tough missions stepped in. Missions that would be embedded in our memories forever.

In 1998, Earl was deployed to Honduras to assist with a natural disaster, an earthquake left many children as orphans. I recall him telling the stories of the ship's crew delivering food to the orphanage and how sad it was. After our phone conversations, I would pray for the children. A few times I dreamed of them. It was at that point I realized Earl's service experiences were invading my subconscious. After returning from Honduras, Earl professed his love for I and my son. He looked deep into my eyes and said "I want to ensure you and Berice are taken care of for life. Will you marry me?"

I immediately felt an obscuring of light from one celestial body by the passage of another creating a source of illumination. My universe changed! February 22nd, 1998 was the happiest day of my life. We got dressed, took a trip to Norfolk's City Hall, and I became Mrs. Delores Pruitt-Polite. I was excited and proud to be the spouse of a Sailor in the United States Navy. God had sent my Boaz!

Rainbow Effects

An alliance is a relationship based on an affinity in interests, nature, or qualities. Earl and I embodied the definition. In 2000, we secured the American dream in Norfolk's historic Bayview area, purchasing a single-family home. I began a career in Corporate America. The routine of Earl frequently being away at sea began to weigh heavily on me.

My husband, partner, and lover were absent from our home. In essence, I had become a single parent. Earl is from South Carolina and I relocated to Virginia from Chicago. There were no family nearby. We missed many holidays, birthdays, and anniversaries together. I experienced many tearful, lonely nights. I was experiencing pure misery! America was on the brink of war with Iraq. Earl was stationed on the USS San Jacinto. During dinner one evening, breaking news came across the television screen announcing that the USS San Jancinto had just launched the first tomahawk missile initiating the infamous war on Iraq. Fear set in. I worried for my husband's safety. Our alliance had officially become complicated.

Earl called home shortly after confirming his safety. Not long thereafter, Earl was pulled from shore duty and deployed to Bagdad, Iraq for seven months. I will never forget how my heart left my chest in the airport as he turned from my embrace to walk through the security check point. My legs gave out on me. God and the airport's floor were my comforter as I wailed uncontrollably screaming for God to cover Earl! The unknown had cast a dark cloud over me. We leaned on coping mechanisms. I threw myself into my career. I was heavily involved in church activities, my son's sports activities, and went to the gym frequently as a stress reliever. Earl took up the hobby of creating Love Song/R&B CD's sharing them with fellow soldiers and working out vigorously. Earl's deployment to Iraq was by far the toughest seven months of our life. Yet, we struggled through it. Earl returned from Iraq different. He spoke of the good experiences and protected me from the bad ones. He heavily boasted about his lunch encounters in Baghdad with Command Sergeant Major James Jordan. He was Michael Jordan's brother and he served in the U.S Army. He often speaks of securing Saddam Hussein's palace and escorting the Navy Chaplin across Baghdad. To-date, his frequent nightmares tell the untold stories of Iraq. The aftermath of serving is the dark side many that serve cope with. They are true heroes.

In 2008, after traveling the world, defending the constitution of the United States of America, and receiving many service metals and awards, my husband retired from the United States Navy after twenty years of service. Our "Complicated Alliance" was nurtured with love, strength, prayer, and faith as small as a mustard seed. For roughly ten years of our marriage, we were together, yet apart. Life after retirement took serious adjustments for the both of us.

As the head of the household with a secure career for the past twenty years, the pressure was on as Earl transitioned into civilian life seeking gainful employment. Earl decided to further his education receiving a Bachelor of Science Degree in Business Management from Saint Leo University. I had become accustomed to taking care of the household independently. Passing the torch was difficult. We both had entered uncharted territory. There were many days I longed for Earl to go back out to sea to avoid us butting heads. Our new normal was challenging.

We were determined to push through and meet the challenges head on. Twenty-three years of marriage gives you the courage to love, to love deep, and unconditionally. Putting what truly matters into perspective brought unspeakable joy to our complex situation. Currently. we are both civilian employees with the Federal Government living our best years together.

Loving and supporting men who serve requires a support system. Family Services are established for all branches of service. They offer great programs specifically outlined to support military families. Leaning on family and close friends provides support while your love one is away serving. Embracing a higher being relieves stress and strengthens your faith.

Our love story is colorful with a plethora of rainy days, resembling a rainbow. **Rainbows** are a symbol of divine anger and patience. Loving a man who has served is indeed complicated. However, the rewards are unmatched. We have secured our pot of gold at the end of our rainbow; each other! My personal experience of the complicity of loving one who has served has bridged an unbreakable alliance. Earl Polite is my hero!

Bio:

Delores Pruitt-Polite is native of Chicago, Illinois and wife to Earl Polite, retired RP1 SW Navy Veteran. Delores entered the corporate workforce as a single parent after relocating to Virginia in 1993. Delores currently serves as a Human Resources Specialist for Military Sealift Command. Formerly, she dedicated ten years of employment to Bank of America as a Unit Manager/Officer of the Bank. Delores embodies hard work and dedication. Following her bliss as a songstress, in 2012 Delores established Phenomenal Sounds Band. Memorable performances include serving as the opening act for a plethora of national recording artists. Delores is a proven philanthropist. She proudly serves the community in various capacities with organizations such as The Reech Foundation and The Edward Myles Foundation. She is the past CEO/Host of Talk is Cheap Radio Show just to name a few. Delores is also a #1 Amazon Best-Selling Author for her anthology, *Undeterred: Success Stories of Female Leaders Who Pursued a Seat at the Table Despite Setbacks.*

deeauthor.com.

DR. DENISE ROBERTSON-LAMBERT

TIED MIGRANT AND CAREER WOMAN

Being a member of the military community is a large part of my life. I was literally born into this world as the daughter of an Air Force Veteran and have served this country in different capacities since then. From a dependent child, to enlisting in the Army National Guard when I was barely out of high school, to marrying an active-duty marine, and becoming the mother of two military dependent daughters; you can say my life has taken a full circle. Anyone who has put on combat boots, or has been married to someone who has, you know military life has many advantages, challenges, and requires tremendous sacrifice. When I decided to marry my marine, I knew that life was not going to be easy. We were young and our first duty station was 3,000 miles away from our parents. But, having said that, the one thing I did not factor into the equation, was just how big the sacrifices would be for me and how negatively impactful this life would have on my professional career aspirations and growth.

Prior to becoming a military spouse, I was a young twenty-year-old, Army National Guardsman, in the process of enrolling in the Reserve Officers' Training Corps (ROTC) program at Hampton University. At the time, I was not sure what degree program I was going to pursue, but I knew I wanted to be an officer and serve in an active-duty capacity in the United States Army. While I completed the initial paperwork for enrollment, I accepted a temporary job at a local fast-food restaurant as a favor to my friend who was a manager. Little did I know at the time, the temporary job would lead to a chance encounter that led to twenty-five years of marriage, two children, and too many relocations to count.

Tied migration occurs when one spouse moves for employment, or career progression, and the other spouse follows (Meadows, Pollack, Karney, & Griffin, 2005). "Tied migrant" is not a title usually associated with the title "military spouse". But, because of the transient lifestyle associated with the military way of life, military spouses are essentially tied migrants. So, as a military spouse and tied migrant, every time my service member received permanent change of station orders (PCS) to another military base, I would resign from my job and remain unemployed until I was able to secure another job at the new duty station; and then the process would begin again two to three years later. When I originally got married, I was in my early twenties and the employment decisions I made along the way, accompanied by the appearance of being a "job hopper" on my resume due to the many relocations, led me, in my mid-forties, to having breaks in my resume, being the recipient of unconscious and conscious biases by hiring managers, career stagnation, under employment, and workplace harassment. In addition, I fell into a category of military spouses that abandoned professional aspirations in exchange for career fields more transferable across state lines and overseas (Alwine, 2021). Even though I have a passion for psychology, I have only pursued employment in the human resources and corporate training industries. The decision to only pursue what I refer to as "safe occupations" has provided me with the ability to quickly gain employment at all duty stations we have been assigned to. But even though I am good at both occupations, I am not excited about them. To date, the jobs I have had just paid the bills. I am not fulfilled by them and I almost feel stuck in the field(s) now due to my age and lack of experience in any other career field or government job series.

Military spouses are often the victims of discriminatory hiring practices that include conscious and unconscious biases that affect hiring decisions and prevents career progression (Manciagli, 2019). Because we are not part of a protected class, finding solutions to hiring discrimination practices, or the intentional underemployment opportunities offered to military spouses, has not been realized. Education is important to me and I was under the impression with more education, I could break through some of the hiring barriers that plague military spouse employment. However, I have been unsuccessful. To date, I have completed four degrees to include a Doctor of Management in Organizational Leadership. And even though I have obtained expert, senior level education and certifications, my career progression has remained stagnant. I remain in entry and middle level positions, even though I possess the skillsets and abilities to perform at a higher level and in a supervisory, senior level capacity.

During one of my interviews, the interviewer asked me how long I would be in the area, and he referenced my employment history which he said let him know I was a military spouse. He was a retired Marine and recognized the locations of residency on my resume. I refused to answer the question and even though I was offered a Senior Instructional Designer position with the organization, the job title did not match the job duties, which consisted of glorified administrative assistant responsibilities. In the end, this retired marine was willing to hire me, but not willing to allow me any real opportunity to contribute since I was a military spouse and he did not know when I would relocate again. It was not lost on me that his conscious bias towards my military status played a part in his hiring decision. Anti-discrimination statutes protect against the bias of an applicant based on age, sex, race, religion, and sexual orientation (Federal Trade Commission [FTC] 2019) but do not protect against the barring of an applicant based on their spouse being a member of the armed forces.

In addition to career stagnation, workplace harassment has plagued my career. Being always the "new girl" at an organization has disadvantages, especially when you possess more education than experience on your resume. And, in some cases, more education than your immediate supervisor(s). Once I am hired within an organization and start demonstrating that I am more capable than my resume may have stated, I begin experiencing workplace harassment in the form of abuse of authority by my immediate supervisors and other bullying tactics they used in an attempt to remove me from the organization. The examples of harassment became worse after I became a doctor. The "Dr." in front of my name created more barriers than opportunities. Instead of receiving promotion opportunities, I was told that my education did not matter and that I did not have enough experience in my resume to warrant promotion or more responsibilities. Imagine putting in so many hours to improve yourself and to make yourself more competitive in corporate America, only to constantly be told that all your hard work is not good enough. Even though I keep a smile on my face, the constant stagnation in my career progression has frustrated me tremendously.

The decision to marry an active-duty service member was the first of many decisions I made that resulted in putting my personal desires on the backburner to support the career progression of my husband's. My story is not unique. I am not the first woman to sacrifice personal goals for the sake of my family. But what I love about my story is that through the struggles, I have remained resilient and determined to move forward and to make lemonade out of the lemons I have been dealt. Through the support of my family and my husband, I have accomplished many of my personal dreams, however, the fight is not over. I often say being a military wife is not for the faint at heart. This life is not easy and is definitely an example of a complicated alliance.

So, one may wonder, why anyone would continue to do this? Why would anyone marry a man in the military at the expense of their own aspirations? Trust me, there have been days when I have asked myself the same question. The answer is simple; I love my husband and he loves me. The family we have built is worth all the sacrifices and, if he received orders today, I would accompany him to the next duty station.

On a personal level, we both do what we can do to lessen the blow of the military way of life to my career. For example, I have recently enrolled in a Diversity and Inclusion training program to increase my knowledge in the field so I can start consulting. In addition, I have started writing books, and contributing to journal articles, and have found opportunities to fulfill my passions while participating in committees with my sorority while giving back to my community. Being a military spouse means that, yes, I am a tied migrant, but it also means I am resilient, flexible, and driven. Until legislation is changed and hiring managers and organizations, start realizing the hidden talents of military spouses, the issues with military spouse employment will continue to be an issue. I just refuse to allow the issue to stop me from being great.

References

Alwine, R. (2021, January 28). Military spouses speak up: We don't just want any job, we want the right job. Retrieved February 14, 2021, from https://www.military.com/2021/01/28/military-spouses-speak-we-dont-just-want-any-job-we-want-right-job.html

Federal Trade Commission. (2019, May 01). Protections against discrimination and other prohibited practices. Retrieved February 14, 2021, from https://www.ftc.gov/site-information/no-fear-act/protections-against-discrimination

Manciagli, D. (2019, January 09). Council post: The MILITARY spouse employment plight. Retrieved February 14, 2021, from https://www.forbes.com/sites/forbescoachescouncil/2019/01/09/the-military-spouse-employment-plight/?sh=73dd863412d1

Meadows, S. O., Pollack, J., Karney, B. R., & Griffin, B. A. (2005). Employment Gaps Between Military Spouses and Matched Civilians. *SAGE Journals*. doi:10.18111/9789284408047

Bio:

Dr. Denise Robertson-Lambert is a government civilian with over 25 years of Human Resources and Program Management experience. She also has a personal relationship with the government as an Army Veteran, the daughter of an Air Force Veteran, the military spouse of a Marine Corps Veteran, and mother of two Marine Corps children. These relationships have provided her with a whole paradigm perspective of the military community.

As part of the findings from her doctoral dissertation, Dr. Robertson-Lambert revealed the effects of unemployment and underemployment on a female military spouses' personal economies, mental health, and job search self-efficacy, which may result in depression and the abandonment of personal goals and objectives for the military spouse.

Dr. Robertson-Lambert has four degrees to include an MBA in Human Resources Management and a Doctor of Management in Organizational Leadership. She is a proud member of Zeta Phi Beta Sorority.

ACCOUNTS

OF

CAREER WOMEN

OF THE

UNITED STATES ARMED FORCES

S'ESTLAVIE KASCHAN BRIDGES

A COUNTRY GIRL WHO BELIEVED SHE COULD

During my sophomore year of high school, I knew I wanted to go to Spelman College. Dance and choreography were always a passion of mine and a natural talent. Spelman was always a college I dreamed of attending to pursue my degree in dance. I applied to Spelman my senior year of high school. Unfortunately, I was not accepted. Talk about a dream crusher! I decided to join the United States Navy. I participated in NJROTC three of my four years of high school and enjoyed it. Just months before my high school graduation, I started the process to join the United Stated Navy. Due to medical issues at the time, I was not able to pass my physical. I was unable to continue the process to join the Navy. Once again, I was left with the feeling of being rejected and having to make a choice on what I would do with my life. I was graduating from high school soon with no plan. In July of 1999, I decided to move to Greenville, SC with my grandparents and attend Greenville Technical College. I went to college for about two semesters and then focused on working full-time since I was technically an adult and needed to take care of myself financially. I could not, nor was I going to, depend on my grandparents who were struggling at the time, to take care of me. The thought of joining the Navy still lingered and was still a desire of mine. After working and living on my own for three years, I decided to try and see if I could still join the Navy. My previous medical issues were no more so there was nothing that would hinder me this time around. I took the leap of faith and embarked on the journey of joining the Navy for a second time around. Everything worked in my favor and on August 29, 2002, I was enrolled in the Delayed Entry Program. Due to the high volume of personnel joining the Navy at the time, I had to wait until my designated date to leave for Basic Training or Boot Camp as we call it. May 7, 2003 was the day I arrived at boot camp and my life was never the same.

Complicated Alliances.......

Currently, I have been in the Navy for eighteen years. Did I ever think I would do as many years as I have? Absolutely not! I joined the Navy for three reasons; to make a better life for myself; obtain money to go to college, and to travel and see the world. I have had the pleasure of achieving all three goals. I came in as an E3, undesignated Seaman; meaning I did not have a specific job, which was my choice because I refused to accept the jobs they offered me. Being undesignated and going to a Wasp-class amphibious assault ship was not what I imagined the Navy to be. I remember the first day I checked onboard, boy was I petrified. The ship was huge to me and the living quarters and amount of space to occupy was unbelievable. In that moment I questioned had I made the right choice in joining. My job consisted of chipping paint, painting the sides of the ship, assisting with underway replenishments, sea and anchor, driving the ship, being a lookout watch stander, inspections, and cleaning constantly. Not what I joined the Navy to do. Five months after checking onboard, I met a Petty Officer First Class who was a Yeoman (YN/Human Resources). She talked to me about the job description and responsibilities. I knew right then, I wanted to be a Yeoman in the United States Navy. 14 months after checking onboard, I was approved to attend YN "A" School in Meridian, MS. YN "A" School was a month long, and I graduated at the top 10% of my class automatically being promoted to Petty Officer Third Class. I always say December 31, 2004 , is the official date I started my career in the Navy. Being in the Navy has afforded me opportunities I do not think I would have been privy to outside of the military, but I have also experienced some not so good moments as well.

Being on two deployments and multiple underways, I have been able to travel to Italy, UAE, Greece, Portugal, India, Japan, Singapore, Kuwait, Hawaii, and various states in the US. The Navy and the many programs they offer have allowed me to obtain my Associate, Bachelor, and Master's degrees without having to use any of my money or take out any loans. The numerous resources available to me day and night, whether it is information on transitioning from one duty station to the next, homeownership, financial or personal counseling, resume writing, parenting classes, financial assistance, or anything else I may need. The Navy can help me for free. There are perks that come with serving in the Armed Forces. I thank God daily for giving me the strength and desire to continue this journey.

Just as I have had some great experiences in the Navy, I have also had some dreadful experiences. Not many people really know what Armed Forces women and men deal with while serving. Each branch is different as well as everyone's experience. I can only speak on mine. First, I will start with the shortage of African American women we have in the Navy. Female Sailor only make up 19% of the population. 8% of that 19% is African American. That proves that the Navy is male dominated and has a great ethnic disparity as well. I have been blessed to make it to the rank of Chief Petty Officer (E-7) and that is a rank in the Navy that is not easy to achieve. It took me sixteen years to get there. If you ask me, I deserved it much sooner, but I realized I made it right on time, "when I was ready for it". I hear from my peers and superiors all the time, "the Navy is looking to diversify the ranks." Yet, the number of African American women in the Navy are still few. Second, as an African American woman in the Navy, I must prove my greatness to others, especially men. Fortunately, for me I am hardworking, motivated, dedicated, a go-getter by nature so I am me always. With that being said, it is a gift and curse. A gift because I can take any task or project, run with it, and produce phenomenal results. A curse because I am viewed by men and some women as having an aggressive personality, being a bitch, or having an attitude. I am one for holding myself and others accountable, regardless of age, gender, or rank. Not everyone likes it nor can handle it. But I have learned I cannot allow other's insecurities or feelings to dictate who I am and what I stand for PERIOD. One thing I preach to my Sailor is to always be true to yourself. Never allow anyone to change who you truly are at the core. I have grown a lot since joining the Navy, especially mentally and spiritually. I can honestly say it was needed. I never look at it as a bad thing because there is always room for growth in everyone, but my prayer is to never change who I am at the core. I was raised by strong women. It took me a little while to find that inner strength but now it just exudes with no effort. That strength is what keeps me going daily; showing up to work ready to train, teach, mentor, motivate, and impact in any way the next generation of Sailor coming behind me. This new generation of Sailor are different. It takes a different type of leadership skill, engagement, understanding, and transparency to reach them.

Lastly, just as racism exists in the civilian sector, it exists in the Armed Forces too. I have never blatantly experienced racism, but there have been times where I knew I was more qualified and more deserving but did not receive the evaluation, award, or position because of my race and gender. I have experienced borderline racist comments from someone not of the same ethnic background as me, while others just ignore or brush it off. I have learned that regardless of how awkward or confrontational it may be, the best way to nip that shit in the bud is to address it. Nine times out of ten the allegations will be denied but they will know going forward that I will not be quiet and stand up for what is right. I genuinely believe if everyone stood up for what was right instead of ignoring the issues, not wanting to get involved, or fear of confrontation, the Armed Forces would be a better environment. That is not just with racism but everything!

Joining the Navy was one of the best decisions I could have made for myself. These last eighteen years of my life have been filled with tears; happy and sad moments, numerous of accolades, accomplishments, and qualifications. An unexplainable joy that only one who has served their country can feel. I was twenty-one when I joined. I was young and not sure what direction I wanted my life to go in. All I knew was that I wanted something better than my current state. I am a better person and leader because of life experiences before joining the Navy, as well as all I have endured while serving. I have no regrets and there is nothing that I would change. My prayer is that I continue to be the leader I always wanted, allow my light to shine regardless of what others may think, hold myself and others accountable, and extend grace always.

Bio:

S'estlavie Bridges was born in Gulfport, MS in 1981. At the age of 3, she moved to Milwaukee, WI with her mother. Due to circumstances of her own, at the age of 13 she abruptly moved to Greenville, SC with her paternal grandparents until she graduated high school. During high school, she enrolled in NJROTC, which sparked her interest in becoming a US Navy Sailor after graduating. Still actively serving, 18 years, she has achieved various promotions, recognitions, awards, and honors, while also completing her Associate,

Bachelor, and Master degrees. Breaking down every barrier that has come her way; S'estlavie is living proof that a woman serving in the Armed Forces is unstoppable.

DR. ZAKIYA O. MABERY

"Behold the One Percenter"

If you are going to be a one percenter, you can't work or think like ninety-nine percent of the individuals in the world. Mindset and mental toughness definitely is required. Be very clear about your dreams and goals, operate with consistency as well as confidence despite the frenemies, haters or naysayers. Perform in your purpose regardless of fear!

What does it mean to be resilient?

Many individuals who have been a part of a military family are adept at meeting others and thrive in certain situations because making connections is natural to them. Military dependents and service members are truly impressive. They adapt to constantly changing neighborhoods and cultures. The variable lifestyle causes military dependents to be strong, flexible, and adventurous. I attended approximately eight schools before I graduated high school. I moved, as an adult, five times due to Uncle Sam. I found inner courage after being the new person or a foreigner in a strange land. Thus, with formal education and my lived experiences I grew into a cultural aware, curious, and courageous diversity, equity, and inclusion (DEI) strategist.

Effective relationships with a few close family members, friends, or others have proven to be quite important. Accepting help and support from those who care about you and will listen to you strengthens resilience. Some individuals find that being active in civic groups, faith-based organizations, or other local groups provides social support and can help with reclaiming hope. Assisting others in their time of need also can benefit the helper I have found.

Being in a military family, you must be okay with letting go some of the control in your life because Lord knows the Army is going to make some big life decisions for you. My father, Troy, missed a father daughter dance once when I was in elementary school in Zweibrucken Germany because he was deployed. My mother, Cheryl, ensured my day was still special. Our chaplain took me. I am such a daddy's girl and appreciate the words of wisdom he has given over the years, like identifying who "got your six" in life. Next year my life partner, Andrew, and I plan on visiting Zweibrucken again soon because we met in third grade in Ms. Sweeney's class. The Army is so big yet so small isn't it? He and I reconnected via social media as adults.

'Let your speech be always with grace', was instilled in me growing in the Army. As someone who speaks to the masses now, I have learned early on in life to always focus first how you address some individuals, second, your choice of words, and thirdly your tone. My father is a retired senior NCO US Army, he has multiple degrees, and taught me the importance of an education. In challenging circumstances, he always contended to respect one's rank or position but recognize that individuals put their pants on one pant leg at a time. Meaning, they are human just like you. I have carried that with me my entire life. Speaking up for my team or identifying gaps in systems or processes was not difficult for me early in my career.

After working in several toxic cultures, I began to experience imposter syndrome and I believed my voice did not matter. As I continue to heal, Andrew and my parents remind me frequently that my tribulations should not affect me assisting others. I have come to realize; my experiences serve as a map for others. When Andrew was the executive officer (XO), I assisted his soldiers who had challenges at times. I was able to do this because of my crystallized experiences. Difficult times strengthen your resilience. Resilience is the ability to cope with a crisis mentally or emotionally; you will return to pre-crisis status quickly. One thing for certain is, my mom often reminds me that change is inevitable. The Army teaches five skills in resilience training which is made up of five pillars. They are self-awareness, mindfulness, self-care, positive relationships, and purpose.

Do you look for opportunities for self-discovery? Both my father and love of my life often remind me to adjust fire when a situation changes. ROTC at VSU taught me "adapting and overcoming" is a key to success as a leader. I have found individuals often learn something about themselves and may find that they have grown in some respect because of their struggles. Many individuals who have experienced adversity, trauma, and hardship have experienced stronger relationships, greater sense of strength even while feeling vulnerable, increased sense of self-worth, a more developed spirituality, and heightened appreciation for life.

Can you relate?

Keeping an optimistic outlook may be difficult if you have a diagnosed mental health condition. I recommend you work with a professional such as a therapist to assist you navigating your past and proceeding towards your destiny. My therapist taught me the value of mindfulness. Practicing mindfulness enables you to focus on the present moment. If you try visualizing what you want, rather than worrying about what you fear, you can begin to see the light at the end of a very dark tunnel. I know this from personal experience. So, take care of your mental and physical health. Pay attention to your own needs and feelings. Engage in activities that you enjoy and find relaxing.

Exercise regularly. Self-care, aids in keeping your mind and body primed to deal with situations that require resilience.

In closing, the official Army colors are **black** and **gold**. **Black** symbolizes knowledge and jurisprudence while **gold** symbolizes achievement and honor. Leaders must lead by example, perform with a commitment to excellence, and assist others in order to achieve true inclusion in the workplace and in our communities.

What modern day symbolism of achievement do you have in your life?

For some it may be a luxury car or the corner office with a view. Others, a stack of degrees or the zip code they live in is a symbol. It is all based off one's lived experiences and upbringing. Hoaah!

Bio:

Dr. Zakiya Mabery a DEI strategist, author, and international speaker who self identifies as an individual with disabilities. Dr. Mabery has written policies at the

Pentagon for The Office of Secretary of Defense (OSD) and walked halls of the White House for official meetings. Dr. Mabery she is an alumnus of two Fortune 500 organizations: Booz Allen Hamilton and Deloitte. Dr. Mabery hosts a digital show called #Gamechangerchat on LinkedIn Live (YouTube) and has an annual summit entitled https://thethrivesummit.net/. Dr. Mabery stresses to her clients and inclusive leaders that one must understand intersectionality and be a change agent. Her distinct perspectives have been shared on some of the world's most prestigious media platforms including Great Day Washington (CBS), Good Morning Washington (ABC), Black News Channel (BNC), KRON 4 News and many more.

TAMIKA QUINN

A SEA BAG, DOG TAGS AND LOVE SAVED ME

My life may look easy and carefree now, but I can remember a time that everything was very difficult and frightening to say the least. As a child, struggling was the norm for us. My mother had me at sixteen years old and we lived with my grandparents. My mother was the baby of seven children, and she lived in a four-bedroom house. Our home was always busy and, in my mind,, very loud as you can imagine. In the living room was a large front window that I would frequently look out of while sitting on the sofa. From that window was a clear view to the train stop directly across the street. The train that stopped there to pick people up and drop people off seemed oddly misplaced to me. Everything around that section of 22nd and Westmoreland St. in my hometown of Philadelphia was run down, except that train.

The train was very nice and the train stop was kept tidy and clean. The train was modern, shiny, and appeared new. It shook our house whenever it came. Sometimes I would run to the living room when I felt it nearing just to see it. Even more odd were the people who rode the train. Many were well dressed carrying briefcases. They would drive their own cars to the train stop and park and ride the train into center city or outside of the city. The people seemed important. I would watch them and wonder where they worked, how much money they made, or what their lives were like. They obviously did not live around here.

Generally, in my daydreaming while looking out of that window, which was quite often, I imagined myself one day boarding that train to get out of my then circumstances. In middle school, my mother got a promotion and moved my siblings and I to a better area in Germantown other than then Mt. Airy. I eventually moved back with my grandmother after getting pregnant at sixteen myself like my mother.

I made a decision that I had to do something different so that I could have something different. I graduated high school even though I had to take my infant son to school with me every day of my senior year. I'm actually thankful for the daycare in the basement of my high school. My grandmother was a huge part of my life. She along with my family, was so proud of me when I graduated. My grandmother was rushed to the hospital right after my high school graduation. I remember standing there with my family in my cap and gown.

My grandmother had a sickle cell attack. She didn't want me to go to the hospital with her. She said you go with your friends; this is your day. Her health seemed to really decline fast after that. One of the last things she talked with me about was really doing something with my life. She was excited that I had taken the ASVAB test and scored pretty high so I could make a choice to go in the Air Force or Navy. I was very hesitant about it and was actually considering college instead. One week after my grandmother passed away, I decided to join the Navy.

That decision came with a steep price. It was the hardest decision I ever had to make, but it certainly wouldn't be my last. That decision required me to go to court and turn over custody of my son to my mother. They told me that you have to be ready and available to serve your country at any capacity and that includes going to war. There was no way I could join the military as a single mother. Someone else had to be responsible for my child at all times. Talk about a loaded decision. I felt like the military was my shiny train that was coming to save me. The decision to join had a hefty price tag.

Although the Air Force was my first choice, they weren't willing to guarantee the medical field for my career choice. They told me that my job would be assigned to me after bootcamp and I thought that was the craziest thing I ever heard. I joined the Navy because they guaranteed me in writing that I would go directly to Hospital Corpsman School after Boot Camp.

My recruiter was young, fine, and I believed him when he told me the Navy was my best choice to get out of Philly. Honestly, he meant out of the hood and that was what I needed to believe in. That belief was like the boarding pass I needed to get on the shiny train in my mind. With an open mind and heart full of hope, one week after my grandmother passed away, I flew from Philadelphia to Chicago in route to begin my journey in the U.S. Navy in Great Lakes, IL. First stop was boot camp. It was the so hard.

I was welcomed by the Chicago winter. Even being from Philly, it was a type of cold I had never experienced. It was cold. I was assigned to Company 94-003. We were only the 2nd group of women to come through Great Lakes Boot Camp. Prior to that, the command had been all men. Just thinking back to that seems unreal that an entire military base could have been made up of one sex seems unheard of these days.

I can assure you that being on that base during that time, women did not receive a warm welcome from everyone. Up until that time, I had never experienced sexism nor racism, but I experienced them both during my time in boot camp. It was definitely a wakeup call to reality for me. It was like I almost grew up overnight. I was not old enough to have experienced integration, but I recall the stories that my mother and grandmother told me about it. I naively thought those days were long over and I would never have to worry about such things. I was wrong. Aside from the rigorous physical horrors of boot camp, there were the mind games. There were lots of mind games. In fact, the entire Boot Camp, looking back on it was one big mind game. Even at the young age of eighteen years old, I found myself in leadership positions when I didn't request to be. During my time there our A-Rock hurt herself and I was quickly assigned to fill in. I held the back of the line up with cadence while marching around the command. At the time, it was not a big deal to me. However, the role was truly significant and spoke volume to characteristics that I have had for a great deal of my life. The military has played a huge role in shaping me into the person I am today. As A-Rock, I remember marching our Unit to the galley to eat one day. There was another Unit's Company Commander at the door. As we marched up to the galley door, he made it very clear that he did not want women in "his galley or his Navy". I was so confused. Respect was being instilled in us, yet we were being totally disrespected by someone superior to us. I didn't know whether to turn our Unit around and march back to our barracks or continue to stand at attention while this man berated us. We waited at attention. He eventually went inside and so did we. My job was to keep time once inside. We had eleven minutes to eat our meals, so you can imagine we ate like scavengers. There was absolutely no talking happening, because there was no time, except for my bellow of "YOUR TIME IS UP". That would signal to the entire Unit to get up, dump their trays, and get in formation to leave. I could not wait to report that incident to the Company Commanders. In my mind, I thought surely, he would be reprimanded or something, but no. My complaints were met with excuses and reasons to sympathize with the crude and belligerent behavior from someone in a leadership position.

    It wasn't all so bad though. I made some lifelong friends in boot camp. I have stories that you would not believe. Some stories I will take to my grave. It seems like we clicked right from the beginning. It was almost like we banned together from the very first day. I remember distinctly because there was one girl, a white girl from Iowa who said out loud that she had never seen black people in real life. Initially I thought she was joking. Who could go through their life never seeing a black person? Unfortunately, she wasn't joking. Later that day she went on a rant that she was being forced to take showers with black people. I watched as the arguments ensued thinking that naturally she will be kicked out. When our Company Commanders were made aware of this girl's racism and other racist remarks, not one thing happened. She was not given any special shower privileges. She also was not reprimanded for her behavior. It was almost identical to the response of the sexist at the galley. I received many lessons during my time in Great Lakes. I will never forget the lessons I received on sexism and racism there.

I spent my first Thanksgiving after my Grandmother's death in Great Lakes. Luckily a friend allowed me and my closest friend at that time, Chanel Hartwell-Williams, to have Thanksgiving dinner with his family in Chicago. It was such a much-needed break. One of the provisions for this special liberty pass was that we had to wear our Navy uniforms to leave the base. We also had a curfew but we didn't care. We did not even care how the food was going to taste. We were so happy to leave that base. His family picked us up. Those four hours were heaven sent.

His family reminded me of the joy in the real world. We laughed with them, looked at pictures, traveled down memory lane with those folks, and ate so much good soul food. I was so thankful. When we left, I cried uncontrollably. I was overcome with emotion. This was the very first Thanksgiving meal that I had in my life that my grandmother had not cooked. It was a raw pain that I had not ever addressed.

I truly had not mourned her death. I ran from it. I knew it was my time to grow up and step up to become the woman God intended me to be. I would go on to serve on the U.S.N.S. Comfort and at Naval Medical Center in Portsmouth, VA. I formed some of the most lasting relationships. None that compared to meeting the love of my life, Casha.

I was working at Portsmouth Naval Hospital. The clinic had received word that a sailor had been injured while out to sea and was being air lifted to the U.S.S. Enterprise. The sailor was airlifted to Germany and then flown to our hospital. To me, it was just paperwork and processing. To my children, it was their life plan.

I remember expecting some really sickly, beat up sailor to be transported in. I remember thinking he does not look like anything is wrong with him. I checked him in. He asked me for my phone number. I said, "What, that is not going to happen". He persisted. I gave him my desk number. We did not know anyone in Virginia yet. He called my work phone and we had small talk. The military begun processing him out for medical reasons. I assumed he would eventually go home. Ironically, he was from Philly. We joked for years that we were from the same place, but he had to travel all around the world to find me.

We talked for a few weeks, then Easter rolled around. He asked if he could ride with me home. He offered to pay for gas going and coming. I thought, "Of course immediately". We rode five hours to Philly. Our conversation was so deep that I met his family that day and he met mine. We were inseparable after that weekend. We have a wedding and two children to prove it.

I say a lot of things about my experience in the Navy. One thing I am forever grateful for was meeting the love of my life. I learned so much in the medical field. I had extensive training that totally prepared me to take care of my husband who battled thyroid cancer and passed away in 2011. The navy also taught me about leadership, a skill that can take you places talent cannot. The Navy was my shiny train and it's one ride I'm glad I took.

Bio:
Tamika Quinn is a two-time Stroke Survivor, Author, Veteran, Widow, Mother of three, Certified Speaker, Award Winning Mentor and Owner of G.L.A.M. Girl, Giving Life and Motivation™. Tamika has been interviewed by Essence Magazine and Buzzfeed to name a few. Tamika has a special place in her heart for helping people avoid stroke and heart disease. She was active in assisting getting the Sodium Warning Label Bill passed into law in her hometown of Philadelphia in 2018. She is a National Spokesperson and volunteer Ambassador for the American Heart Association and currently serves as the American Heart

Association's Chair of the Legislative Policy Committee. Tamika is the Author of "Change Your Mind, Change Your Waistline" and Co-Author of "The Woman Behind The Mask". Both can be found on Amazon. Keep up with Tamika online at www.TamikaQuinn.com, Facebook @authortamikaquinn and Instagram @fatgirl2glamgirl.

THERESA CARPENTER

SWITCHED NAVY CAREER THREE TIMES, FOUND MY CALLING

In sixth grade, I wrote stories to make sense of my world and describe my innermost thoughts and feelings. Miss Susan Byrnes, my sixth-grade teacher, assigned our class to keep a journal that she reviewed each week. She encouraged me to write by telling me I could articulate ideas cohesively. For the next couple of years, I kept numerous spiral bound notebooks and would jot down ideas, and when I was feeling deeply expressive, I wrote poems. None of this was intended for public consumption, but more to help me think clearly about my experiences using a creative outlet. When I was in the eighth grade, we had a career day where industry professionals met with us to talk about their vocations. Based on my love of writing, I choose to meet with a news reporter. That day, as I was sitting with that journalist from the Columbus Dispatch and listening to him describe his day-to-day duties, I was enthralled. I thought I'd become an investigative journalist. Little did I know I would spend twenty years working in careers as far away from storytelling as possible, to then one day get back to an industry that in my childhood was calling me.

After that day with the reporter, I immersed myself in other endeavors such as backstage crew for our high school theater productions or flag corps. I had stopped writing. My parents noticed my strong sense of empathy for others, and due to me being adopted and understanding the feelings of being unwanted, I considered becoming a social worker. A few years later, when I was sixteen, I decided that working and earning a livelihood was priority. I had started to lose sight of my passions and by the time I joined the Navy at nineteen, the fire for writing or social work was out.

In the Navy I became an aviation electrician's mate and I was responsible for rewiring electrical systems for the Navy's S-3B Viking, an anti-submarine warfare aircraft. I became proficient at performing basic maintenance functions, as I could always be depended on to launch and recover aircraft on the flight deck. I became the go-to person in my work center and racked up numerous technical qualifications such as starting up the engines at a high-power setting or running the auxiliary power unit. Based on my qualifications and experience, our civilian technical representative selected me as his assistant. I was qualified on every piece of equipment that he needed operating to help him troubleshoot a maintenance discrepancy.

I excelled at briefing our maintenance chief petty officers the status of the electrical issues and our team's plan for fixing them. The command leadership took noticed of my abilities. As a result, they encouraged me to submit an officer package. They saw leadership potential in me. I lacked the vision to imagine what job I wanted as a naval officer, but after consideration and thought, perhaps moving up through the ranks and getting a college degree through an officer program would help me figure it out. I decided to apply for the Nurse Corps Program remembering my goal of becoming a social worker and I figured I was destined for a helping profession.

The Navy had other plans for me. To my delight, my application for a commission was accepted. However, instead of becoming a nurse, I was given three Navy Warfare areas options: surface, aviation, or nuclear. After meeting a Navy journalist when I was attending an officer preparatory school, I choose surface warfare. While chatting with her, my passion for writing was rekindled.

Memories came flooding back on how much I enjoyed writing and communicating with others through stories. She told me the Surface Warfare Officer community was the easiest community to laterally transfer to another officer community. After attending the preparatory class, I decided to major in communications and gain experience with the hopes of one day leaving the SWO community and becoming a Public Affairs Officer.

There were no guarantees that going into the SWO community was going to lead to public affairs. However, I was entering a warfare community that I wasn't thrilled about with no assurances that it would lead to what I eventually wanted. However, I was determined that if there was even a small chance that I could get accepted into Navy public affairs, it was worth it for me to take this route.

After graduating from college with a major in communications and an internship at a local newspaper, I headed off to Pearl Harbor, one of the Navy's most beautiful and tropical climates. I began qualifying as a SWO on USS Russell (DDG 59), a guided-missile destroyer. It was a fervent work pace for that year and half learning about the ship's weapon systems, the engineering plant, and how to drive a million-dollar warship. It was in this assignment I met my first mentor in public affairs; the civilian public affairs officer for Navy Region Hawaii. She let me coordinate numerous Pearl Harbor commemorative events. I had an incredibly supportive command leadership who empowered me to run a robust marketing program on the ship. I learned how to operate a camera, design a newsletter, and wrote numerous articles on the ship's and crew's activities.

My commanding officer supported my desire to switch careers but knew my current officer community wasn't letting anyone go as they wanted to keep as many as possible in my year group. He wisely advised me to put an application package as it would show me how to build my portfolio. In addition, it would send a signal to the PAO community that I was a viable candidate should later my officer designator allowed people to laterally move.

After being onboard my ship for a year and due to an influx of junior officers needing to get qualified, I got the opportunity to be temporarily assigned to a large headquarter command to learn my craft at a more operational level. I had no idea if this experience would help me get selected to public affairs, but I knew if I didn't even try, I'd never know if it was possible. After not being selected the first time I applied, I continued to polish my portfolio and the following year submitted another application package for public affairs.

In the meantime, I ran the command's Distinguished Visitor Program, which sent out community leaders for a day at sea on our aircraft carriers. It was a transformative period because I now knew there existed a path for me in the Navy, but I still had no assurances I would get selected. After more than ten years working through the system, I could only hope I'd one day have a career that capitalized on my unique talents merging my passion with my paycheck.

I was at my desk when the email came announcing that I was selected into Navy public affairs. As tears rolled down my face, I realized that all my hard work had finally culminated into a job that would tap into my creative side. I burst into my boss's office and profusely thanked him for giving me the opportunity to practice being a PAO before the official selection. I knew from that day forward my career would never be the same. Instead of planning my separation from the Navy, I was going to continue serving well past twenty years in a job that I could be promoted in and love doing.

With the months I've spent away at sea far from loved ones, I always wanted a vocation that didn't feel like work. To be fair, even in the public affairs community, there are days that are incredibly challenging. Despite the hard times, I love being a Public Affairs officer and believe in the mission of telling the military story. At times I push through difficult periods with the help of mentors who are instrumental in guiding my journey. I'm glad I never gave up on my dreams on getting a vocation that capitalized on my strengths. I'm thankful that I worked in the Navy Aviation and Surface Community first, as it's given me a unique perspective into those career fields I'd never have seen firsthand otherwise. My time as an enlisted sailor helps me relate to our most junior members, as I was once in their shoes, not sure if I wanted to make the military a career or do my required first enlistment and leave.

My advice to others who are not sure of their career path is to examine what they enjoy when earning money is *not* the priority. It's vital to find a vocation or profession to capitalize on one's strengths. We have a personal brand that distinguishes us from others. I mix my creative side using my skills in public affairs tactics with a strategic end game. I start every plan with a rough idea of where I want to end up. The experience taught me that just because one is in an unsatisfying career doesn't mean you're stuck there. I never settled for the career that was chosen for me and by rekindling my passion I got back to where I always belonged.

Bio:

Theresa Carpenter is an active-duty Navy Lieutenant Commander where she has served for the past twenty-five years. Her passions include helping military women succeed and the professional development of the craft of public relations. As an introspective writer, she muses about the human experience for her blog, Theresa's Tapestries. Tapping into her love of storytelling through the visual medium, she runs a RWeCrazy, YouTube channel, with her husband where they share their experiences with saving money, DIY projects, traveling, and enjoying time together. She lives in Norfolk, Virginia with her husband Harry and their Boxer dog Jayda, who also has her own social media presence on Instagram. Set to launch this summer, her podcast, Stories of Service (S.O.S.), will showcase ordinary people doing extraordinary work in all walks of life.

APPENDICES

Complicated Alliances.......

OTHER BOOKS BY THE VISIONARY DR. KAREN HILLS PRUDEN

Complicated Alliances.......

OTHER BOOKS BY THE VISIONARY DR. KAREN HILLS PRUDEN

UNDETERRED

Success stories of female leaders who pursued a seat at the table despite setbacks

DR. KAREN HILLS PRUDEN

OTHER BOOKS BY THE VISIONARY DR. KAREN HILLS PRUDEN

ATTRACT, THEN REPEL: WHY ARE CANDIDATES ABANDONING YOUR EMPLOYMENT PROCESS?

Dr. Karen Hills Pruden, SPHR

Complicated Alliances…….

OTHER BOOKS BY THE VISIONARY DR. KAREN HILLS PRUDEN

OTHER BOOKS BY THE VISIONARY DR. KAREN HILLS PRUDEN

Complicated Alliances.......

OTHER BOOKS BY THE VISIONARY DR. KAREN HILLS PRUDEN

Complicated Alliances.......

OTHER BOOKS BY THE VISIONARY DR. KAREN HILLS PRUDEN

SPEAKING MY TRUTH
Book Anthology

Dr. Karen Hills Pruden — Co-Author

Cheryl Wood — Visionary

amazon.com BEST SELLING BOOK

OTHER BOOKS BY THE VISIONARY DR. KAREN HILLS PRUDEN

Complicated Alliances…….

OTHER BOOKS BY THE VISIONARY DR. KAREN HILLS PRUDEN

COURAGEOUS ENOUGH TO Launch!

OPEN

STORIES & STRATEGIES OF EVERYDAY WOMEN WHO FACED THEIR FEARS TO LAUNCH & GROW THRIVING BUSINESSES

DR. CHERYL WOOD

amazon.com BEST SELLING BOOK

Made in the USA
Columbia, SC
14 April 2021